W9-AFV-100

DISCARD

GREAT PREDATORS

GRIZZLY BEAR

by Jody Jensen Shaffer

Content Consultant
Bruce D. Leopold, PhD
Sharp Distinguished Professor of Wildlife Ecology
Mississippi State University

CORE
LIBRARY

Published by ABDO Publishing Company, PO Box 398166, Minneapolis,
MN 55439. Copyright © 2014 by Abdo Consulting Group, Inc.
International copyrights reserved in all countries. No part of this book may
be reproduced in any form without written permission from the publisher.
The Core Library™ is a trademark and logo of ABDO Publishing Company.

Printed in the United States of America,
North Mankato, Minnesota
052013
092013

Editor: Lauren Coss
Series Designer: Becky Daum

Library of Congress Control Number: 2013932506

Cataloging-in-Publication Data
Shaffer, Jody Jensen.
 Grizzly bear / Jody Jensen Shaffer.
  p. cm. -- (Great Predators)
ISBN 978-1-61783-948-1 (lib. bdg.)
ISBN 978-1-62403-013-0 (pbk.)
Includes bibliographical references and index.
1. Grizzly bear--Juvenile literature. 2. Bear--Juvenile literature. 3. Predatory
animals--Juvenile literature.   I. Title.
599.784--dc23

                                    2013932506

Photo Credits: Scott E. Read/Shutterstock Images, cover, 1; Shutterstock
Images, 4, 10, 41, 43, 45; age fotostock/SuperStock, 8; Animals Animals/
SuperStock, 13; Stock Connection/SuperStock, 15; iStockphoto, 16; Andre
Anita/Shutterstock Images, 18; Gleb Tarro/Shutterstock Images, 20; Bruce
& Jan Lichtenberger/SuperStock, 22; Cusp/SuperStock, 25; David Rasmus/
Shutterstock Images, 26; Design Pics/SuperStock, 28; Red Line Editorial,
30, 40; Thinkstock, 32; Exactostock/SuperStock, 34; Mat Hayward/
Shutterstock Images, 36; Peterson Media/Shutterstock Images, 39

CONTENTS

CHAPTER ONE

GETTING TO KNOW THE GRIZZLY BEAR

It's spring. A grizzly wakes from hibernation. He is desperate for food. He lifts his nose and smells bison. It's the season for bison calves to be born.

The grizzly follows his nose to a bison herd. Adults forage on young plants. Calves play nearby. In the safety of the herd, the bison are safe from the bear. But one calf has wandered away from the herd. The grizzly makes his move. The bear begins chasing

Grizzly bears are the top predators in their habitats.

the calf. The mother bison runs in between her calf and the bear, trying to protect her baby. But the grizzly is much faster than the calf. It separates the baby bison from its mother. Then the grizzly's sharp teeth grab the calf. His long claws hold it. Eventually, the mother bison runs to safety without her baby.

Bear Basics

Grizzly bears live in the northwestern continental United States, Alaska, and western Canada. They range in color from light brown to black. Their thick hair is nearly white at the tips, making them look grizzled, or gray. This feature gave grizzlies their name. The hair insulates

Grizzly or Black Bear?

Black bears are another common species of bear in North America. Grizzly bears are sometimes confused with black bears. Grizzlies are bigger than black bears. Grizzlies have a hump of muscle on their shoulders. Black bears don't have this hump. Black bears have shorter, more rounded muzzles than grizzlies. Black bears also spend much more time in trees than grizzly bears.

the bears, keeping them warm during the cold winter months.

Grizzly bears are very large animals. Male grizzlies average 300 to 860 pounds (136–390 kg). Most females weigh 200 to 450 pounds (91–204 kg). Most grizzlies that live in the continental United States stand between six and eight feet (1.8–2.4 m) tall. Kodiak bears, grizzlies that live only in parts of Alaska, are even bigger. Some Kodiak bears can weigh 1,500 pounds (680 kg) and stand up to ten feet (3 m) tall. Grizzlies are known for their sharp teeth and long claws.

Despite their great size and power, grizzlies have small facial features. Their ears are short and rounded. Grizzlies use

Hollywood Grizzly

One of the most famous grizzlies was a nine-and-one-half-foot (2.9-m) tall, 1,500-pound (680-kg) bear named Bart. Bart was born in 1977 in a Baltimore, Maryland, zoo. Doug and Lynne Seus adopted the bear. They trained Bart to be in movies and on television. Bart appeared on-screen more than 20 times. Bart died from cancer in 2000.

Grizzlies spend much of their time snacking on nutritious plants.

their long muzzles and sensitive noses to sniff out prey. They use their good hearing and eyesight to protect their cubs from danger.

Grizzly bears are talented predators. They may eat other animals when they are fattening up for winter. But they don't eat only meat. Much of their diet comes from berries, grasses, and roots.

In the early 1800s, explorers Meriwether Lewis and William Clark first told the world about grizzlies, which they called white bears, through the journals they kept of their expedition to the West:

> We saw also many tracks of the white bear of enormous size, along the river shore and about the carcasses of the buffalo, on which I presume they feed.
>
> We have not as yet seen one of these animals, though their tracks are so abundant and recent. The men, as well as ourselves, are anxious to meet with some of these bear. The Indians give a very formidable account of the strength and ferocity of this animal, which they never dare to attack but in parties of six, eight, or ten persons; and are even then frequently defeated with the loss of one or more of their party. . . . This animal is said more frequently to attack a man on meeting with him, than to flee from him.

Source: "To the Yellowstone." The Journals of Lewis and Clark. University of Virginia, 2007. Web. Accessed March 25, 2013.

Consider Your Audience

Review this passage closely. How would you adapt it for a different audience, such as your parents or younger friends? Write a blog post conveying this same information for the new audience. How does your approach differ from the original text and why?

CHAPTER TWO

THE LIFE OF A GRIZZLY

Female cubs begin reproducing when they are six or seven years old. They will have cubs of their own every four years or so. Male and female grizzlies mate between May and July. Grizzly bears have many different mates throughout their lives.

Some females mate with more than one male in a given mating season. Not all the fertilized eggs inside the female's body will grow to be cubs, however. If

Most female grizzly bears give birth to twin cubs.

the female grizzly can't find enough food to support her pregnancy, the eggs won't grow. Before having her cubs, the female grizzly needs to fatten up for the winter. She will have her cubs while she is hibernating.

Hibernation

Grizzlies eat a lot in the summer and fall to store up fat for their winter hibernation. Some experts believe grizzlies must eat up to 40,000 calories a day, resulting in a five- to six-pound (2–3-kg) weight gain per day. By the fall, a grizzly may weigh 85 percent more than it did in the spring.

In the fall, grizzly bears look for a place to hibernate for the winter. They may make a den under rocks, in the hollow of a tree, or in a hillside.

Hungry as a Bear

Have you ever been as hungry as a bear? It's not likely. On a normal day, grizzlies can eat up to 20,000 calories of food. That's like a human eating 40 hamburgers and 40 ice cream sundaes in 24 hours! And when the bears are preparing for hibernation, they can eat twice that amount. Grizzly bears' go-to foods are berries, pine nuts, and fleshy roots.

Grizzly bears make dens to spend the winter in.

They use their long claws to dig their dens. They make a bed of branches and leaves inside.

The first grizzlies to enter their dens in the winter are pregnant females. Females with one- to two-year-old cubs enter next. Solitary males and females enter their dens last. When grizzlies leave their dens in the spring, they do so in reverse order.

Grizzly bears don't enter a true state of hibernation. In true hibernation, an animal's heart rate drops drastically. The animal almost stops breathing completely. Its body temperature plunges to within a few degrees of freezing. Grizzlies enter a modified hibernation, often called carnivore lethargy. A bear's heart rate decreases. Its metabolism drops. Its body temperature declines a few degrees. But unlike true hibernators, grizzlies will wake up if they are disturbed or hungry.

Cubs

Pregnant females give birth in their dens in January or February. They usually have between one and four offspring. A set of twins is the most common number of offspring.

Newborn cubs have very little hair. They are toothless and blind. They don't open their eyes for up to three weeks. Grizzly newborns weigh approximately one pound (0.5 kg) and are the length of a piece of notebook paper. The cubs snuggle up to their sleepy mom and drink her milk. Newborns

Grizzlies and their cubs stay in their dens all winter. When spring comes, the bears leave their dens to search for food.

Grizzly bear cubs wrestle with one another.

spend the rest of the winter in their den, growing and drinking.

When spring arrives, the mother and her cubs make their way out of their den. The mother bears are usually a little sluggish. They weigh much less than they did when they entered their dens. The cubs, on the other hand, are full of energy. They run and jump on each other. They fight and play.

The cubs weigh approximately five pounds (2 kg) now. They still rely on their mother's milk for nourishment. The family usually stays close to their den for a few weeks. Once they leave the area, the cubs remain by their mother's side. Keeping her cubs safe is a mother grizzly's most important goal. She will fight to the death to protect them.

Grizzly Grunts

Grizzly bears communicate with one another using different sounds. Grizzlies growl, roar, and grunt to frighten predators away from their cubs. The mother grizzly also communicates with her cubs using moans or grunts. She uses these noises to warn her cubs of danger. Grizzlies also communicate by rubbing their bodies against trees. This leaves the grizzlies' smells, so other bears know the bears have been there.

Growing Up

During the next two to four years, the mother grizzly teaches her cubs everything they need to know to

Mother grizzlies teach their cubs how to hunt and survive, but eventually the cubs need to go off on their own.

survive. She shows them how to protect themselves, how to dig a den, and how to find food. Eating takes up most of their time. The bear family may spend 16 hours a day eating.

When grizzly cubs are between one and four years old, they separate from their mothers. This separation usually occurs when the mother is ready to mate again. In areas with little food, the cubs may stay with their mother longer. Sometimes cubs are reluctant to leave their mothers. Their mothers may have to chase them off.

This is a dangerous time for young grizzlies. They don't have their mothers to protect them. They might not be familiar with the area. Many cubs become prey for male grizzlies or wolves. Some sources suggest that less than half of all grizzly cubs make it to adulthood. The cubs that do survive can live for up to 25 years. Grizzly bears can live up to 50 years in captivity.

EXPLORE ONLINE

The focus of Chapter Two is a grizzly bear's life cycle. The chapter also discusses young grizzlies. The link at the Web site below discusses grizzly bear cubs. As you know, every source is different. How is the information on the Web site different from the information in this chapter? How is the information the same? How do the two sources present the same information differently?

Grizzly Bear Cubs
www.mycorelibrary.com/grizzly-bear

CHAPTER THREE

PREDATORY TRAITS

Grizzly bears are powerful predators at the top of their food chain. They chase, kill, and eat animals, including rodents, squirrels, moose, elk, caribou, deer, and fish. Grizzlies in Alaska eat a lot of salmon. Sometimes grizzlies prey on domestic animals, such as cows and sheep. Coastal grizzlies may dig up and eat clams.

Grizzly bears fish for salmon as the fish make their way upstream.

Kodiak bears eat a dead seal on Alaska's coast.

Grizzlies hunt prey that is easy to catch, like young or elderly animals. They also steal caribou or moose that other animals have already killed. When they've had their fill, grizzlies store the leftovers under a pile of leaves to return to later. Grizzlies are omnivores. They eat plants and animals.

Built for Hunting

Despite their large size, grizzlies are fast and fairly nimble. They can run 30 miles per hour (48 km/h) for short distances. They can even climb trees to chase prey. Grizzlies are also strong swimmers.

A grizzly's body is made to do heavy lifting. In its strong jaws, a grizzly can carry a 300-pound (136-kg) sheep down a mountainside. It can topple a 700-pound (318-kg) trash container. A grizzly can lift a huge boulder with one paw in its search for food underneath.

Grizzlies' teeth and claws make their speed and strength even more terrifying for possible prey. Grizzly bears have canine teeth two inches (5 cm) long. These teeth are perfect for biting and holding on to prey. The bears can also catch fish with these powerful teeth.

Claws four inches (10 cm) long also help grizzlies catch and kill their prey. Grizzlies use their claws for scraping bees from their hives. They also use claws for making dens and digging

The Buzz on Honey

Bears are famous for liking honey. But bears actually would rather eat bees and their larvae than their honey. Grizzly fur is thick enough that it is tough for a bee to sting a grizzly bear. But for grizzlies, the protein rich larva is worth getting stung. Beekeepers in bear country build fences around their hives to keep them safe from bears. Many fences are electrified.

Super Sniffers

Grizzly bears have very sensitive noses. Their sense of smell is their most important sense. Grizzlies can smell humans several hours after they have hiked a trail. They can smell newborn elk, which are thought to be nearly odorless. They can smell dead animals miles away.

up roots and small creatures.

Grizzly Senses

All of these specialized predatory traits wouldn't help if grizzlies didn't have great senses to go with them. Grizzlies especially rely on their keen sense of smell. They use their noses to locate prey and juicy berries. They sniff the air to sense nearby enemies. Some scientists estimate that a grizzly's sense of smell is seven times better than a bloodhound's and 2,100 times better than a human's. It is the grizzly's most valuable sense.

Grizzlies also have excellent eyesight. They can see objects nearly 200 feet (61 m) away. That's the length of five school buses parked end to end. Most experts think grizzlies can even see in color.

Grizzlies use their powerful noses to track down food.

A grizzly's hearing is a little better than a human's. Humans hiking in bear country should be sure to make lots of noise. This gives grizzlies time to run away before the hikers reach them. It's never a good idea to surprise a grizzly bear. Hikers who do surprise a grizzly, especially a mother with cubs, will likely be greeted with a ferocious growl. The bear may charge.

During certain times of the year, grizzlies may be fiercer than at other times. As they prepare for hibernation in the summer, they need lots of food, especially pregnant females. After hibernation,

Grizzly bears' excellent senses help them catch their prey.

grizzlies are equally desperate for food. Mother grizzlies need to eat for themselves and for the cubs they are nursing. Grizzlies are more likely to be aggressive when they are hungry or protecting cubs.

Naturalist Douglas H. Chadwick has studied grizzly bears for many years. In 2001 he describes an encounter with a grizzly in an article for *National Geographic*:

> *Climbing an October mountainside in Montana's Glacier National Park, I notice a grizzly about the same time it notices me. . . . It begins eyeing me—a sidelong check now and then. It's enough to make me suddenly remember how many of my footsteps to get here landed in craters. Digging for roots nonstop as den-up time nears, this creature has torn half the face off a mountain. One more glance from the bear, with the wind and my pulse roaring louder in my ears, and I veer down toward timberline, on bear-raked soil all the way.*

Source: Douglas H. Chadwick. "Grizz." National Geographic 200.1 (2001). EBSCOhost. Web. Accessed April 12, 2013.

What's the Big Idea?

Take a close look at this passage. What is Chadwick's main point? Pick out two details he uses to support his main point. Write a few sentences about how he uses these details to support his main point.

CHAPTER FOUR

RANGE AND HABITAT

Grizzly bears are a subspecies of brown bear. Brown bears live in the Northern Hemisphere from Europe to Asia to North America. At one time, grizzly bears freely roamed the open and unpopulated land of North America. In the early 1800s, an estimated 50,000 grizzly bears lived between the US Pacific Coast and the Great Plains in the center of the United States. This area included

Grizzly bears are most common in Alaska and western Canada, but some still live in the western continental United States.

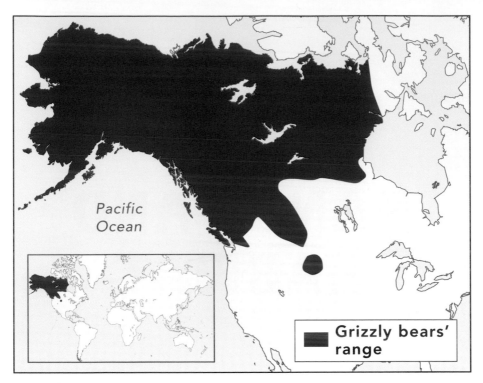

Grizzly Bears' Range

This map shows the grizzly bears' range. After reading about their habitat, what do you imagine it looks like? Why might this area be well-suited to grizzly bears? What characteristics help grizzlies survive in these areas?

sandy coastal beaches, gigantic mountain ranges, thick forests, and miles of grasslands and flat prairie.

Then Europeans began settling the West. They needed room for homes, businesses, and crops. They needed space for their livestock to graze. The grizzly's range became smaller and smaller. Thousands of grizzlies were killed, and their numbers plummeted.

Thanks to conservation efforts, grizzly populations are increasing across North America. Today grizzlies live in western Canada, Alaska, Yellowstone National Park, and Glacier National Park in Wyoming and Montana. Some grizzlies live in the Selkirk Mountains of Idaho and Washington and the Cabinet-Yaak area of northern Idaho.

At Home with Grizzlies

Grizzly bears often prefer habitats near rivers and streams, so they have easy access to fish and fresh water. Each grizzly has a territory. Grizzly

Staying Safe around Grizzlies

What safety tips should you follow when hiking in grizzly bear country? There are no hard-and-fast rules, but following these guidelines should help keep you safe:

- Remain calm if you see a grizzly.
- Slowly step away from the bear while still facing it— never run away.
- Speak to the bear in a calm tone.
- Always hike with other people, not alone.
- Get your bear spray ready.
- Ask local park rangers and law enforcement about bear activity in the area where you are hiking.

Grizzly bears live in huge territories, which they often guard from other bears.

territories are huge. They can be hundreds of miles long and thousands of acres in size. Another grizzly may occupy a grizzly's territory. But only if the first grizzly allows it, which it may do if food is plentiful and no cubs are present. Grizzlies leave messages indicating who owns a territory. They scratch trees and rub against them, sometimes leaving tufts of fur behind. They urinate on the ground as a warning to other bears.

The grizzly bear's habitat is varied and depends on the season and availability of food. In the spring and fall, grizzlies move to lower elevations near streams, rivers, meadows, and grasslands. In the summer, early fall, and winter, they live at higher elevations with fir trees and boulder fields. They feed, rest, and make their dens in timbered areas.

FURTHER EVIDENCE

There is quite a bit of information about the grizzly's range and habitat in Chapter Four. What do you think is the main point of the chapter? What evidence was given to support that point? Visit the Web site below to learn more about this topic. Choose a quote from the Web site that relates to this chapter. Does the quote support the author's main point? Does it make a new point? Write a few sentences explaining how the quote you found relates to this chapter.

Grizzly Bear Recovery
www.mycorelibrary.com/grizzly-bear

CHAPTER FIVE

THREATS TO THE GRIZZLY

Adult grizzly bears don't have natural predators except other grizzlies. These massive animals are well equipped to protect and care for themselves. Grizzlies also don't have much competition for food. Because of their size and the variety of things they eat, grizzlies get the first pick of plants, animals, and anything else that looks good.

Humans building roads and cities on former grizzly habitats is one of the greatest threats to grizzly bears.

People camping in bear country should make sure they pack any food in bear-proof storage containers to keep out any hungry grizzlies.

Bear and Human Harmony

The greatest threat to grizzlies is humans. Homeowners leave garbage and livestock unprotected. Sometimes landfills fail to secure their borders. This gives grizzlies easy access to food. Once they've learned where a source of food is, grizzlies use their great memories to return to it again and again. This puts humans and grizzly bears in more frequent contact, which can be a problem.

Sometimes homeowners or ranchers kill nuisance grizzlies. Wildlife officials may try to catch and remove the bears from human areas. But removing grizzly bears usually fails.

Grizzly bear attacks on humans are rare. But they can happen when a human surprises a grizzly, especially a mother bear with cubs. Hikers should always talk to local law enforcement or park rangers to learn about any bear problems that may have occurred along an area's trails.

Hikers should be sure to make noise when walking through bear country. A bear's sharp hearing will detect that humans are coming. Hunters and hikers should also carry bear spray. This

When Bears Attack

Unfortunately, bears sometimes attack humans. There are two kinds of bear attacks on humans, predatory and defensive. A predatory attack is when a bear stalks its prey, usually from behind, to kill and eat it. A defensive attack is when a bear attacks a human to protect cubs or because it has been surprised. Most grizzly attacks on humans are defensive.

is a spray that humans can use to stop an aggressive bear. The spray is painful for the bear but will not permanently injure it.

Hunting

In 1975 the US Fish and Wildlife Service listed the grizzly bear as a threatened species in the lower 48 states under the Endangered Species Act. This placed grizzlies under federal protection from hunting and trapping. It is still legal to hunt grizzly bears in Alaska and Canada. But strict laws are in place to make sure hunting doesn't threaten the grizzly population. States monitor grizzly bear numbers to make certain their population stays about the same

Yellowstone Grizzly Bears

Yellowstone National Park in Wyoming and Montana was established in 1872 as the first US national park. In 2007 grizzlies in Yellowstone National Park were taken off the Endangered Species list, though their numbers are still monitored closely. Now Yellowstone's grizzlies are some of the park's most popular sights.

Today Yellowstone National Park is one of the best places to spot grizzly bears in the continental United States.

or increases. This hard work has paid off. Experts believe there are more than 1,000 grizzly bears in the lower United States and up to 25,000 grizzlies in Canada. Alaska has the highest grizzly population with between 25,000 and 40,000 bears.

However, illegal poaching still occurs. Poachers knowingly kill animals that are protected by law. The poachers' customers pay hundreds of dollars for grizzly bear teeth or other parts.

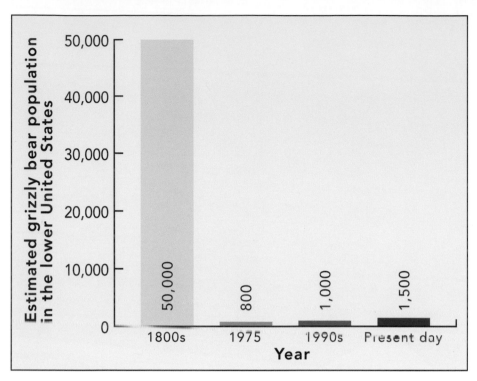

Grizzly Bear Population over Time

In the 1800s, no scientific studies were done to track grizzly bear populations. People had to estimate their numbers. By 1975 only 800 grizzlies remained. Their numbers improved in the 1990s. This graph shows how grizzly bear populations changed in the United States over time. What might have happened to change the bears' population over time?

Protecting the Grizzly

Several organizations work hard to protect grizzly bears and to help humans and grizzlies coexist. The National Park Service, the US Fish and Wildlife Service, and the US Forest Service cooperate to save grizzlies. The state governments of Washington,

Setting aside protected habitat for grizzly bears helps keep their populations from falling further.

Idaho, Montana, and Wyoming are involved as well. These groups conduct studies and promote strategies to save grizzlies. They regulate human land use that could threaten grizzly habitat, such as mining. The organizations also help set aside land outside of national parks so grizzlies can have more habitat untouched by humans.

The National Wildlife Federation, the Great Bear Foundation, and many other conservation organizations also help with recovery efforts. Lots of caring, knowledgeable people want to ensure that grizzly bears stay around for a long, long time.

Common Name: Grizzly bear

Scientific Name: *Ursus arctos horribilis*

Average Size: Six to eight feet (1.8–2.4 m) tall

Average Weight: Males usually weigh between 300 and 860 pounds (136–390 kg); females usually weigh between 200 and 450 pounds (91–204 kg)

Color: Light brown to black; fur is often nearly white at the tips

Average Life Span: 25 years in the wild

Diet: Plants, such as leaves, berries, and grass; meat, including rodents, squirrels, moose, elk, caribou, deer, and fish

Habitat: Conifer forests, wooded areas, dry grassland, and near rivers and coasts across northwestern North America

Predators: Humans and other grizzly bears

Did You Know?

- Grizzlies that live in the lower 48 states are generally smaller than those in Alaska and Canada.
- Grizzlies walk with their feet flat on the ground like humans.
- Grizzly bears can spot objects up to 200 feet (61 m) in the distance.

STOP AND THINK

Say What?

Studying grizzly bears can mean learning a lot of new vocabulary. Find five words in this book that you've never heard before. Use a dictionary to find out what they mean. Then use each word in a new sentence.

Dig Deeper

After reading this book, what questions do you still have about grizzlies? Maybe you want to know more about grizzly bear conservation. Or maybe you want to know where grizzly bears live. Write down one or two questions that can guide you in doing research. With an adult's help, find some reliable sources about grizzlies that can help answer your questions. Write a few sentences about what you learned from your research.

Why Do I Care?

The grizzly bear population in the United States has declined greatly over the past 200 years. Even if you don't live near grizzly bears, why should you care about their decline? What might their decline mean for the future of grizzlies and other animals?

You Are There

This book discusses how grizzlies sometimes roam onto private property where they are not protected. Imagine you are a rancher whose cattle have been attacked by grizzlies. What would you do?

GLOSSARY

conservation
management of natural
resources for continued use

domesticated
not wild

endangered
an animal that has become
rare and is in danger of dying
out completely

expedition
a journey taken for a specific
reason

ferocious
extremely fierce

forage
search or graze for food

hibernate
pass the winter in a resting
state

nourishment
food

omnivore
an animal that eats plants and
animals

species
a group of similar animals
that are closely related
enough to mate with one
another

subspecies
a type of animal in a
geographic area with physical
characteristics slightly
different from those of other
animals in its species

LEARN MORE

Books

Lang, Aubrey, and Wayne Lynch. *Baby Grizzly*. Markham, ON: Fitzhenry & Whiteside, 2006.

Sartore, Joel. *Face to Face with Grizzlies*. Washington, DC: National Geographic, 2007.

Shapira, Amy, and Douglas H. Chadwick. *Growing Up Grizzly: The True Story of Baylee and Her Cubs*. Guilford, CT: Falcon Guide, 2007.

Web Links

To learn more about grizzly bears, visit ABDO Publishing Company online at **www.abdopublishing.com**. Web sites about grizzly bears are featured on our Book Links page. These links are routinely monitored and updated to provide the most current information available.

Visit **www.mycorelibrary.com** for free additional tools for teachers and students.

INDEX

ABOUT THE AUTHOR

Jody Jensen Shaffer is a poet and the author of 12 books for children. She writes from the home she shares with her husband, two children, and dog in Missouri.